Lynda's Baby

Lynda's Baby

Written by Sharon Koble

Illustrated by Jay Holladay

XULON PRESS

Xulon Press
2301 Lucien Way #415
Maitland, FL 32751
407.339.4217
www.xulonpress.com

© 2020 by Sharon Koble
Illustrated by Jay Holladay

All rights reserved solely by the author. The author guarantees all contents are original and do not infringe upon the legal rights of any other person or work. No part of this book may be reproduced in any form without the permission of the author. The views expressed in this book are not necessarily those of the publisher.

Unless otherwise indicated, Scripture quotations taken from the English Standard Version (ESV). Copyright © 2001 by Crossway, a publishing ministry of Good News Publishers. Used by permission. All rights reserved.

Paperback ISBN-13: 9781631295843
Hard Cover ISBN-13: 9781631295850
Ebook ISBN-13: 9781631295867

My life, as well as this book, is dedicated to the original author of this story, my Lord and Savior, Jesus Christ.

"Now to Him who is able to do far more abundantly than all that we ask or think, according to the power at work within us, to Him be glory in the church and in Christ Jesus throughout all generations, forever and ever. Amen."
– Ephesians 3:20-21 ESV

With many thanks to Craig and Seth for your encouragement, support, encouragement, love, encouragement, prayers and did I mention encouragement? Thank you to my greatest prayer warrior – my mom. I love you all so much! Thank you, Jay, for bringing color and life to these pages. And last, but not least, thank you to the Hollinger-Janzen family for allowing me to put your story on paper. I can't wait to see how God will use this book!

I first met Lynda on December 14, 1993. She was serving as a missionary in Cotonou (KOH-tun-OO), Benin (Ben-NIN), a small country in West Africa. Her office was in the maternity ward of a healthcare center. While there, she met many moms and newborns. One newborn, however, was special. This is the story Lynda told me about that special baby...Lynda's baby.

Lynda was working on some paperwork in her office when a doctor rushed in and startled her.

"Someone just brought in an abandoned baby!" Dr. Honorine (Own-er-EEN) announced nervously. "What are we going to do?"

The doctor explained that the baby had been found in a park and was brought to the hospital by someone who heard him crying. She told Lynda that the baby's tiny left leg bent inward instead of being straight. Lynda hadn't even seen the child yet, but immediately, she heard God say, "This baby is for you."

Emotions flooded over her. Lynda and her husband, Rod, hadn't been thinking of adding to their family. They already had two children and Lynda had just started a new job. Still, Lynda couldn't shake that feeling. She talked with her husband, and together they decided they should keep the baby with them for a short time until there was room in the local orphanage. So Lynda swaddled the baby, hopped on the back of a motorcycle taxi, and took him home. Rod and their daughters, Mimi and Rachel, were delighted to see the baby and very excited to help take care of him.

Friends stopped by to welcome Lynda's baby. Some began calling him Moïse (Moe-EEZ) because his rescue reminded them of the story of baby Moses in the Bible.

Another friend looked at the tiny child and said, "You would not have survived if God didn't love you. We should call you Oluwafemi (Oh-LOO-wah-FEM-ee) because it means God loves me."

Rod and Lynda thought that was perfect, so they named the baby Oluwafemi Moïse.

Several weeks passed and the orphanage was still full. Lynda's family continued to take care of Oluwafemi who was quickly becoming a part of their family.

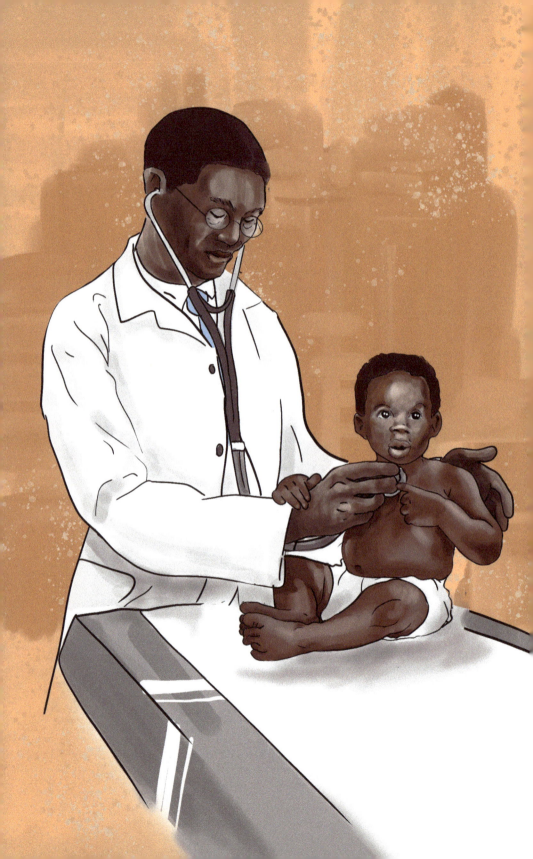

Lynda and Rod knew it was time to find out what could be done for the baby's crooked leg, so they took Oluwafemi to see a special doctor. After the examination, the doctor told them that the baby might never be able to walk. He felt the best thing to do would be to place him in a body cast for six months and *hope* that it would help straighten his leg. This was not what they wanted to hear.

Lynda and Rod had some decisions to make. Their family was scheduled to return to the United States soon, and they would be gone from Africa for three months. They knew they could not take Oluwafemi with them because legally, he was not their child. What would they do with the baby while they were gone? What should they do about his crooked leg?

A kind family from their church in Benin offered to take care of the baby while Lynda and her family were in the United States. But if they did, Oluwafemi would not be in a body cast as the doctor had suggested.

"We will keep him, but not in a body cast," they explained. "We will pray, and you will see what God will do."

Lynda and Rod understood that many women in Africa carry their little ones on their backs, making it easier for them to work. If Lynda's baby were in a cast, her friend would not be able to carry him on her back.

Although they knew Oluwafemi's leg might not heal, they agreed to let this family care for him while they were gone.

By the time Lynda's family returned to Benin, Oluwafemi had learned to stand and move around. At ten months, he began to walk! Over time his crooked leg gradually straightened, and by his fourth birthday, there was no problem with his leg!

"It was God's intervention," Lynda said. "We prayed for God to heal the leg, and God did."

Lynda's baby, now a young boy, was five years old when Lynda and Rod legally adopted him. A short time later, they left Africa and moved to the United States.

Oluwafemi had no trouble getting used to his new life in Goshen, Indiana. His outgoing and friendly personality helped him to make friends quickly and adjust to the different culture.

Oluwafemi continued to grow into a healthy and very energetic boy. It wasn't until he started going to school that his energy became somewhat of a problem. At times he would get "in trouble" because sitting still was just so hard for him. His body needed to move. His parents began taking him to a local gym before school so he could run two miles, just to burn energy.

In his free time, Oluwafemi found the perfect outlet for his need to move – soccer. Both of his parents enjoyed soccer, and so did his friends in Benin. While in Africa, his friends taught him how to play, and Oluwafemi caught on to the sport quickly.

What began as just a playtime activity for him, soon turned into his passion. He spent hours dribbling a soccer ball and practicing his kicks. He grew strong physically and became very skilled at the game. No other sport captured his heart and soul like soccer.

He played in local soccer clubs and, as a freshman, became a starter on his high school team. Oluwafemi finished his high school career with 67 goals, a school record, and 23 assists. He was named the 2011 Gatorade Indiana Boys Soccer Player of the Year and the 2011 Indiana Player of the Year!

Oluwafemi's dream was to play soccer in college, but where? He knew college coaches would scout, or look, for good players that they wanted on their team. Since his high school was very small, not many college coaches had noticed him. He decided to make a list of colleges that he thought he would like to attend. He also made a list of his "dream schools." These were the schools that were known for their winning soccer programs, but Oluwafemi didn't think he would have a good chance to play for them. Indiana University, IU, was one of his dream schools. When his family learned of a soccer camp at IU, Rod thought his son should attend.

"If the big schools aren't coming here to scout you, why don't you just go to the big schools?" Rod asked his son.

But Oluwafemi was feeling discouraged, so he put off signing up for camp. However, his dad was more hopeful. While Oluwafemi was traveling on spring break, Rod noticed that the soccer camp was filling up quickly, so he decided to send in his son's registration himself. It just so happened that one of the last spots for Indiana University's soccer camp went to Oluwafemi!

From day one of soccer camp, Oluwafemi stood out. He was motivated to play his best because he knew college coaches were watching. Finally, this was his chance to get noticed! He gave his best effort and worked hard all week. By the end of camp, Oluwafemi had earned the camp's Most Valuable Player award! But that's not all… IU's soccer coach wanted him to play for Indiana University's soccer team!

Oluwafemi was thrilled! He was awarded a soccer scholarship and was able to attend Indiana University, one of his dream schools! He was a starter for the Indiana Hoosiers all four years and helped them win a National Championship during his freshman year. And just think, Oluwafemi almost missed going to soccer camp!

After college, Oluwafemi's dreams continued to come true. He was drafted by the New England Revolution and became a professional soccer player! By the way, remember all that energy that used to get Oluwafemi in trouble? Well, his coach said he liked his energy!

Despite everything Oluwafemi achieved in soccer, he remains humble. He knows he's been blessed and that life could have been very different for him. He says it's his faith, family, and others who have supported him that made him a better person and soccer player. He's learned that it's important to dream big, work hard, stay positive, and never give up.

"When I look back on things, I would not be where I am today if I had not been adopted. I think God has a plan for everyone in life. God had a definite plan for me," Oluwafemi says.

Lynda had no idea that she would be a part of that plan when she went to Africa as a missionary. I sure am thankful she did.

I'm thankful I met Lynda in that healthcare center on December 14, 1993.

I'm thankful she listened to God's voice that told her, "This baby is for you."

I'm thankful Lynda and Rod chose to adopt that abandoned baby with a crooked leg.

I'm thankful that friends in Benin taught that squirmy little kid with too much energy how to play soccer.

And I'm thankful Rod got that discouraged high school soccer player into soccer camp.

I'm thankful because this is *my* story and that kid, Lynda's baby, is me! My name is Oluwafemi Moïse Kotounou (Koh-TOO-noo) Hollinger-Janzen.

But you can call me Femi.

CPSIA information can be obtained
at www.ICGtesting.com
Printed in the USA
LVHW071221230720
R160746000001B/R160746PG661205LVX1B/1